W9-CLG-617

TINY
BUDDHA'S
INNER STRENGTH JOURNAL

Creative Prompts and
Challenges to Help You Get
Through Anything

LORI DESCHENE

CITADEL PRESS
Kensington Publishing Corp.
www.kensingtonbooks.com

CITADEL PRESS BOOKS are published by

Kensington Publishing Corp.
119 West 40th Street
New York, NY 10018

All Kensington titles, imprints, and distributed lines are available at special quantity discounts for bulk purchases for sales promotions, premiums, fund-raising, educational, or institutional use.

Special book excerpts or customized printings can also be created to fit specific needs. For details, write or phone the office of the Kensington sales manager: Kensington Publishing Corp., 119 West 40th Street, New York, NY 10018, attn: Sales Department; phone 1-800-221-2647.

CITADEL PRESS and the Citadel logo are Reg. U.S. Pat. & TM Off.

ISBN: 978-0-8065-4223-2

First Citadel hardcover printing: September 2022

10 9 8 7 6 5 4 3 2 1

Printed in the United States of America

ISBN: 978-0-8065-4224-9 (e-book)

INTRODUCTION

This is just a season, not a lifetime. I've gotten through hard times before. Something good may come from this, I just can't see it now.

These are all things I've told myself when life has felt impossibly hard—when it's seemed like the odds have been stacked against me, and I've felt drained and overwhelmed and scared . . . scared to face the day before me, scared of what's coming down the line, scared that things may never feel easy or good or safe again, as if they ever really have.

That's the thing about challenging times—we never know how long they'll last or if there will ever be a time when we feel we've made it to the other side. We can never know for certain what the future will hold; the only thing we can know for sure is that we have the strength to handle it and even make the best of it, whatever it may entail.

It sounds simple enough: When you find it hard to have faith in anything, hold on to faith in yourself. When you can't trust that everything will be okay, trust that *you'll* be okay, because you have inside you everything you need to not only survive, but also thrive.

But what if you don't believe that? What if you feel weaker than you've ever been, or you've always felt weak, so it's hard to believe you'll ever feel anything but? What if you know you're strong, but it seems like everything that's working against you is stronger? How do you find the will to keep going when it feels like you never really get anywhere, no matter how hard you try?

As someone with a history of PTSD, depression, and bulimia, I've felt these things many times before. I've questioned not just my will to go on but also my capacity. I've assessed all my experiences and choices and concluded there was something wrong with me—*that's* why I struggled so badly—which meant I was doomed to fall into the same painful patterns, and even worse, I may have deserved it.

But I've recognized something over the past many years of navigating challenges big and small. Since I started Tiny Buddha in 2009, I've learned a lot about what it takes to rise up and keep going when I want to roll over and hide. As I've grappled with loss and disappointment, watched others suffering while feeling powerless to help, and carried more pressure-filled responsibility on my shoulders than I ever imagined I could, I've realized I've become someone *who can deal.*

Once upon a time, at the first sign of trouble, the people around me worried I would fall apart and hurt myself. Because that's generally what I did. And to be fair, sometimes I *still* fall apart—I collapse into a chocolate-stained heap of sheets, crying the kind of heaving, guttural tears that feel primal and draining and raw. But then I get back up, because I now have the tools to calm my mind and manage strong emotions, and I prioritize self-care as best I can, so I feel firmly rooted in my power when life's tornadoes threaten to take me down. I still struggle to apply what I've learned at times, but I now believe I am strong, because I've acted from strength many times before, and that belief pulls me through even when I don't feel it.

That's what this journal is all about. The pages that follow reflect the ideas, habits, and exercises—many backed by research—that have helped me get stronger and believe in myself even when I've felt weak and lost. And not just me, but countless Tiny Buddha blog contributors. More than two thousand people have shared their stories over the years, many detailing awe-inspiring accounts of crisis and resilience. Illness, addiction, abuse, and loss—the blog reflects the full gamut of human suffering and our immense capacity to heal and emerge on the other side of pain stronger, wiser, and better off for having gone through it. This journal incorporates the many recurring lessons and insights you'll find scattered throughout the blog. It represents a holistic journey to nurturing inner strength, categorized in four sections—mental, emotional, physical, and spiritual—because it all works together to build us up into our most powerful selves. That's what enables us to stand tall when the unexpected tries to knock us down, as it inevitably will.

Each of the four main sections includes seven subsections, with writing prompts, a doodle prompt, and a challenge in each. Though you don't need to work through each page chronologically, I recommend completing one subsection before shifting gears, and ideally focusing on one of the main four categories at a time. This way, you'll build momentum and create meaningful change in one area of your life before moving on to another. If any of the prompts or challenges don't feel relevant or helpful to you, feel free to rewrite them to suit your own needs. The only thing that matters is that you use this journal in a way that empowers you. There's no right or wrong, no deadline, no pressure, and no ending to arrive at—just a book of ideas for exploration and experimentation, each page a step on a never-ending journey.

It's likely this journal has found its way into a vast array of hands—some of them aged and worn from years of hard work and struggle, and some less visibly battered but overwhelmingly full nonetheless. Though I don't know your unique story, I know you've been through your own version of hell and that you're a survivor, even if you don't always feel like it. Something inside you has pulled you through, even when your fears and beliefs have tried to hold you back. I hope this journal helps you reinforce and build upon all the strength you've already fostered so that next time you tell yourself a million reassuring things to help you carry on, you believe them—because you fully believe in yourself.

Building Inner Strength Mentally

There's no denying that our circumstances can feel devastating at times. Still, much of our experience of the world stems from what goes on in our minds—and oftentimes, it's highly disempowering. We tell ourselves we can't do hard things, and then everything feels a lot harder. We convince ourselves that nothing will ever change and then never change anything as a result. We dwell on the negative, expect the worst, and focus on problems instead of solutions. As a result, we feel bad about ourselves and our lives—and why wouldn't we? How could we possibly feel confident and hopeful when our mind tells us all the reasons we shouldn't? We can't control all our thoughts—they often pop into our head without conscious choice, which means it's futile (and exhausting) to try to stop "negative" thinking. But we can consciously choose what we think and believe about ourselves and our lives—and feel a lot stronger as a result. That's what this section is all about.

The following pages cover seven different types of mental habits that can either empower or drain us:

- **Assessing your strengths and weaknesses,** so you can recognize, celebrate, and nurture your strengths and change how you perceive your weaknesses instead of getting down on yourself for having them.
- **Developing a growth mindset,** so you can recognize your potential to grow and improve over time instead of assuming you're forever doomed or limited in certain areas of your life.

- **Changing your interpretations,** so you can learn to focus on what's going well and what's possible instead of bemoaning what's wrong and fearing the worst.
- **Keeping things in perspective,** so you're able to find blessings in disguise and stay hopeful in difficult situations, knowing that nothing is forever and very little is as bad as it seems.
- **Changing your perception of change,** so you can turn fear and resistance into excitement and acceptance, which helps you face the future with confidence, knowing you can handle and even enjoy whatever is coming down the road.
- **Releasing disempowering beliefs**, so you're not limited and weakened by beliefs about who you are, what you can do, what you deserve, and how the world works.
- **Focusing on solutions**, so you can stop dwelling on things you can't control and take responsibility for what's within your power, enabling you to better adapt to change and cope with hardship.

This section is really about the lens through which you view yourself and the world, each exercise one stroke toward cleaning away the mud that darkens your perspective. You're stronger than you realize, you can do more than you think, and you have more possibilities than you know—now grab your pen and prove it.

ASSESSING YOUR STRENGTHS AND WEAKNESSES

Remember the time you thought
you could never survive? You did,
and you can do it again.

–UNKNOWN

List below what you believe to be your top strengths, one way you've used each of them recently, and why you feel proud of yourself for each of these experiences.

_____

_____

_____

_____

_____

_____

_____

_____

_____

_____

_____

What are your top accomplishments, and what strengths did you use to achieve them?

I'd like to get stronger at _____,
and I could do that by ...

_____

_____

_____

_____

_____

_____

_____

_____

_____

_____

_____

_____

Identify your greatest weakness and one way it could actually be a strength. For example, you may believe your sensitivity is a weakness, but it has enabled you to empathize with people you love. See if you can activate this "strength in disguise" today and then write about what the experience was like for you. Fulfilling? Empowering? Why or why not? Did you have any epiphanies about yourself?

Explore below what your life would look like if you never judged yourself or put yourself down for your weaknesses. What might you do differently? How might this affect your state of mind? Your work? Your relationships?

_____

_____

_____

_____

_____

_____

_____

_____

_____

_____

_____

_____

Draw a heart—broken in multiple pieces—and in each piece write a wound from your past and one strength you gained as a result.

DEVELOPING A
GROWTH MINDSET

Sometimes you get what you want.
Other times, you get a lesson in
patience, timing, alignment, empathy,
compassion, faith, perseverance,
resilience, humility, trust, meaning,
awareness, resistance, purpose, clarity,
grief, beauty, and life.
Either way, you win.

—BRIANNA WIEST

Write about something you've improved at over time through hard work, consistency, and dedication. It could be something work-related or personal—any area of your life where you struggled at first, but then saw progress after allowing yourself space to learn and grow. List anything that helped you improve and anything you learned about yourself through this experience.

What's an area of your life where you're currently holding a fixed mindset—telling yourself you're bad at something and you can't change or improve because your traits and talents are set in stone? What would you do differently if you didn't believe this was true? And how might this change your feelings about yourself and your life?

I may have failed at _____,
but through this experience I learned . . .

_____

_____

_____

_____

_____

_____

_____

_____

_____

_____

_____

Today, ask someone for constructive criticism on anything important to you, and practice seeing it as something positive—an opportunity to learn, grow, and improve, instead of something you need to take personally and use as evidence that you're not good enough. Note below what criticism they gave you and what you can take from their feedback.

Imagine you're having dinner with your inner critic and they're telling you all the reasons you can't do something hard that you really want to do, and why you shouldn't even try. Write a script in which they share their reasoning, and you offer empathetic, reassuring objections to each point to prove their fears and beliefs aren't facts.

Write the word "yet" in large block or bubble letters and fill them with decorative patterns. Around the word, write all the hard things you want to do but haven't done or don't know how to do yet, to reinforce that you can do these things in time.

CHANGING YOUR INTERPRETATIONS

Sometimes when things are falling apart,

they may actually be falling into place.

—J. LYNN

Write about a time when you feared the worst possible scenario, but then things turned out for the best, or better than you expected. Note how much time you spent worrying, how this affected and possibly weakened you, and what you learned from the experience.

_____

_____

_____

_____

_____

_____

_____

_____

_____

_____

_____

_____

What's one challenge you're currently facing, and how might it actually be an opportunity?

Though it hurt at first, it was a blessing in disguise when . . .

_____

_____

_____

_____

_____

_____

_____

_____

_____

_____

_____

_____

Today, whenever something causes you distress, ask yourself, "How might this be happening *for* me, not *to* me? What gifts might this challenge bring me?" Then write about what happened. What good did you find in your struggles, annoyances, or conflicts? How did this new way of thinking about your struggles affect your mental state and your day?

_____

_____

_____

_____

_____

_____

_____

_____

_____

_____

_____

Look outside your window and identify one thing you could easily interpret negatively—the weather, a seemingly difficult person, a traffic jam. Then write a short story in which this negative is actually a positive, as a practice in seeing challenges from a more empowering angle.

_____

_____

_____

_____

_____

_____

_____

_____

_____

_____

Draw an ocean with many waves, each representing a negative thought you hold about yourself or your life that might seem like a fact. Write those thoughts in the waves as a reminder that you just need to ride them out instead of attaching to them and letting them pull you down.

KEEPING THINGS
IN PERSPECTIVE

You have to stop thinking you'll be stuck in your situation forever. We feel like our heart will never heal or we'll never get out of this impossible struggle. Don't confuse a season for a lifetime. Even your trials have an expiration date. You will grow, life will change, things will work out.

—BRITTNEY MOSES

Think about one or two little things that are currently weighing you down and write about why they won't matter five days, five weeks, five months, or five years from now.

Have you ever experienced something that you thought would dramatically impact your life, but it ended up not being a big deal in the grand scheme of things? What happened, and what did you learn from the experience?

If I were to choose my battles wisely, I would no longer get worked up about . . .

_____

_____

_____

_____

_____

Instead, I would . . .

_____

_____

_____

_____

_____

Today, whenever something stresses or annoys you, shift your focus to one thing you can appreciate about the experience—for example, the time to listen to a podcast when you're stuck in traffic. Write about your experience at the end of the day. What did you appreciate? How did this affect your mental state? Did this impact how you showed up in the world in any way?

_____

_____

_____

_____

_____

_____

_____

_____

_____

_____

_____

Imagine you're lying on your deathbed, looking back at all the worries that never materialized and all the problems you were fortunate not to have. What advice would an older you give your current self to help you keep things in perspective?

Draw all the things in your life you can enjoy and celebrate even if things aren't perfect.

CHANGING YOUR PERCEPTION OF CHANGE

Change is hard at first,
messy in the middle,
and gorgeous at the end.

—ROBIN S. SHARMA

Write about how you would adapt and even grow stronger if you lost your current means of financial support.

_____

_____

_____

_____

_____

_____

_____

_____

_____

_____

_____

What's the scariest change you've ever faced, and what are some ways you grew and benefited from the experience?

Change can be exciting and empowering because . . .

_____

_____

_____

_____

_____

_____

_____

_____

_____

_____

_____

_____

Today, make three minor changes to your routine. For example, complete a difficult task first thing in the morning, or enjoy some time outside when you would usually relax indoors. Or if you're feeling bold, make one to three big changes, to strengthen your adaptability muscle. Then write about what you did differently and what this experience was like for you.

Think about someone you know who's made a positive change even though it was scary. How might their life have progressed if they'd stayed in their comfort zone and avoided this change?

_____

_____

_____

_____

_____

_____

_____

_____

_____

_____

_____

Draw a tree with leaves falling to the ground. In each falling leaf, write one thing you've lost. Then, for each one, draw a corresponding leaf on the tree with something you gained from that loss.

RELEASING DISEMPOWERING BELIEFS

Promise me you'll always remember:
You're braver than you believe,
and stronger than you seem,
and smarter than you think.

—A.A. MILNE

List one to three negative beliefs you hold about yourself, your life, or the way the world works—beliefs that bring you down and make you feel less capable of thriving and/or handling what's coming down the road. For each, write one reason this belief might not be true, and if possible, offer evidence from your past experience (or someone else's) to support this.

_____

_____

_____

_____

_____

_____

_____

_____

_____

_____

_____

Who or what most influenced your beliefs about your ability to handle adversity, and what might you believe instead if you hadn't known those people or had those experiences?

If I believed I could handle anything, I would . . .

_____

_____

_____

_____

_____

_____

_____

_____

_____

_____

_____

Think of something you've wanted to do—something to better yourself or improve your life—that you don't believe you can. Ask someone who believes in you why they think you can do this and detail their reasoning below. Do you believe what they said? Why or why not? What would need to change for you to see yourself through their eyes, and move forward with this goal?

Pick one disempowering belief about yourself, your worth, or your capabilities and write about a day in your life if you gave that belief the day off.

Design a tattoo around the word "strong," and draw it on the part of the body where you'd place it, as a reminder that you can do and handle hard things. If you don't love the idea of inking up your skin, imagine it's a temporary henna tattoo.

FOCUSING ON SOLUTIONS

Incredible change happens in your life
when you decide to take control of what
you have power over instead of craving
control over what you don't.

—STEVE MARABOLI

Think of an area in your life where you're currently struggling. List your top fears about this situation, and next to each fear, write one thing you could do to adapt or cope if that fear came true.

_____

_____

_____

_____

_____

_____

_____

_____

_____

_____

_____

_____

What's the biggest challenge you've ever faced? How were you able to overcome it, despite your obstacles and feelings? What qualities, skills, or choices enabled you to find a solution?

_____

_____

_____

_____

_____

_____

_____

_____

_____

_____

If I focused more on solutions than problems, I would stop ...

_____

_____

_____

_____

_____

and start ...

_____

_____

_____

_____

_____

_____

Today, notice any time you're tempted to blame someone or something else and instead, focus on finding a solution to the problem. Write about what this was like for you. Who were you tempted to blame, and why? What solutions, if any, did you identify? How did it impact your day and your mood to focus on problem-solving instead of pointing fingers?

Write a breakup letter to worrying, explaining why worry doesn't help you solve your problems and what you intend to do to help yourself whenever worries start weighing you down.

_____

_____

_____

_____

_____

_____

_____

_____

_____

_____

_____

_____

_____

Draw yourself blowing bubbles from a wand. Then, using author Dona Sarkar's "100 bad ideas" framework, think of as many "bad" ideas as possible to solve a problem you're currently facing, and write each one in a bubble in the sky above you. Don't worry if your ideas are ridiculous. You might be surprised by the good ideas that emerge when you take the pressure off and let your imagination run wild!

Building Inner Strength Emotionally

Most of us live our lives at the mercy of our emotions, without fully understanding what we're feeling and why, and it's incredibly painful and draining. We just feel and react, or numb and distract because we were never taught how to identify our feelings and work through them in healthy ways. We also devote a great deal of energy to avoiding emotional discomfort, whether that means blaming other people to avoid taking responsibility for our lives, hiding from things we fear, or hiding from other people to avoid potential judgment. And ironically, we judge ourselves through all of it, as if our emotions are signs of weakness. As a result, we feel bad *and* feel bad about feeling bad—not a great foundation for navigating hard times. It's like breaking our own legs before walking through a hurricane; we're set up to fail from the start. But our emotions don't have to be a liability; they can be a source of strength if we change how we relate and respond to them. That's what this section is all about.

The following pages cover seven different types of habits that help us build emotional stability and resiliency:

- **Developing emotional awareness,** so you can understand, process, and consciously respond to your emotions instead of letting them overwhelm you and reacting in ways that disempower you.

- **Nurturing self-compassion,** so you can love and support yourself through challenging times instead of beating yourself up and dragging yourself further down.
- **Adopting an internal locus of control,** so you can take ownership of the things within your control instead of feeling powerless and placing blame on everyone and everything else.
- **Fostering optimism,** so you can see the good in the bad and hold on to hope for the future, which can help you keep going when life gets hard.
- **Facing your fears,** so you can courageously face the things that scare you instead of letting them control you, define you, or hold you back.
- **Embracing vulnerability,** so you can share your feelings with other people, which helps you release them, along with the shame that keeps you feeling small and stuck.
- **Accepting emotional discomfort,** so you can learn to sit with uncomfortable feelings and then let them go, instead of distracting or numbing yourself and keeping those feelings trapped in your body.

This section is essentially about owning your emotions instead of allowing them to own you. It's about embracing your shadow while creating the light you need to see your way through dark times. It's also about learning to pause between feeling and acting so you can respond from a place of power and awareness. No matter what you feel in any given moment, there is a place of calm knowingness deep inside you that can help you make wise, empowered choices. Take a deep breath, grab your pen, and get ready to explore it.

DEVELOPING
EMOTIONAL AWARENESS

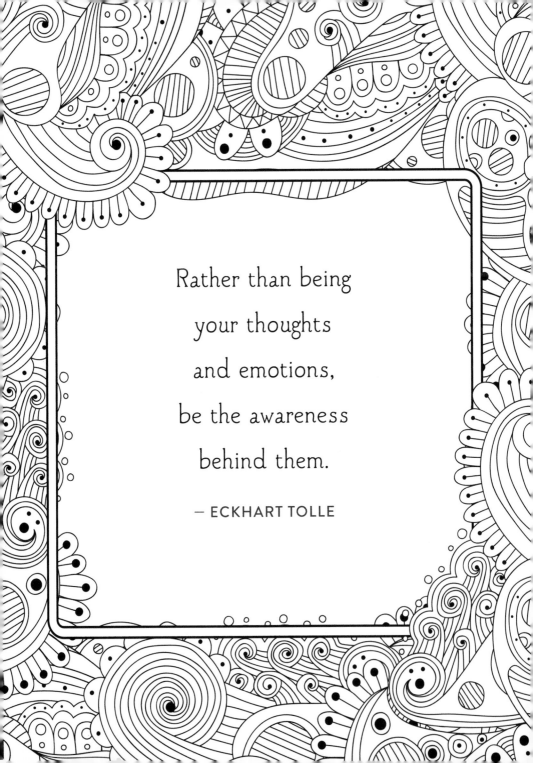

Rather than being
your thoughts
and emotions,
be the awareness
behind them.

— ECKHART TOLLE

Think of the last time you experienced a strong emotion and complete the prompts below to help you understand your feelings, the consequences of your reaction, and how you can respond differently next time this emotion takes hold.

Emotion you felt:

_____

Why:

_____

How you reacted:

_____

What the consequences were:

_____

What you might do differently next time:

_____

_____

Who or what have you blamed for your feelings recently (thinking they made you feel insecure, angry, etc.)? What's the payoff of blaming them? What do you gain? What can you avoid acknowledging, accepting, or doing by blaming them? And what would you do differently if you considered that you alone are responsible for how you feel and how you respond to your feelings?

_____

_____

_____

_____

_____

_____

_____

_____

_____

_____

I am more apt to respond to life emotionally when I . . .

_____

_____

_____

_____

_____

_____

I can increase the odds of responding more calmly and rationally
by . . .

_____

_____

_____

_____

_____

Identify and write down your feelings here throughout today, without judging them and before acting on them. Note what triggered the feeling or feelings—a thought, judgment, fear, or perception of someone else's behavior. Get curious about each one and observe them without trying to fix them. See how this pause for reflection defuses the intensity of your emotions and allows you to respond from a calmer, wiser, more empowered place.

Try to identify the source of one of your strongest emotional triggers—a memory/wound from childhood that causes you to react strongly when you experience something similar as an adult (e.g., feeling ignored, underestimated, rejected, judged, etc.). Write a letter to your younger self, offering compassion, comfort, and support to help your inner child feel safe, seen, and free to let go of any beliefs that no longer serve them.

Draw yourself in a protective bubble that represents your emotional boundaries. Outside the bubble, jot down any feelings you've been tempted to take on as your own that belong to other people—for example your partner's sadness or your coworker's anxiety. Let this be a reminder that you don't need to feel or fix anyone else's feelings or allow them to dictate your own.

NURTURING
SELF-COMPASSION

Empowerment is realizing you are the one who needs to say the things you've waited your entire life to hear.

—MATT KAHN

Make a list of all the things you do and say to yourself that you would never do or say to someone you love. For each, write what you would do and say to that person instead.

_____

_____

_____

_____

_____

_____

_____

_____

_____

_____

_____

What pressures and expectations can you let go to feel more balanced and less stressed? What would it look like if you went through your day tomorrow without their weight pulling you down?

I forgive myself for . . .

_____

_____

_____

_____

_____

_____

_____

_____

_____

_____

_____

_____

Before every meal today, or any time you're feeling down on yourself, look in the mirror and tell yourself something compassionate you need to hear. For example, validate your feelings, acknowledge that you're doing your best and that your best is good enough, or forgive yourself for a mistake. Write about what this was like for you. Were these messages comforting and helpful? If not, why? And what would need to change for you to believe those self-compassionate words?

Imagine yourself standing in front of two doors. One leads to your future if you face your greatest struggles with self-compassion going forward; one leads to your future if you continually beat yourself up and act from a place of shame and disempowerment. What do you see when you open each door?

_____

_____

_____

_____

_____

_____

_____

_____

_____

Imagine if the quality you least like about yourself had a physical form. Draw yourself hugging or holding hands with this quality and write around the drawing any words of acceptance or appreciation that come to mind.

ADOPTING AN INTERNAL LOCUS OF CONTROL

At any given moment,

you have the power to say:

This is not how the story is going to end.

—CHRISTINE MASON MILLER

Think of a situation (or more than one) that is currently stressing, worrying, or overwhelming you. List the things you feel are outside your control, and for each, one thing that is within your power, to reinforce that you always have choices. For example, maybe you can't leave your job, but you can choose to somehow make it more enjoyable.

_____

_____

_____

_____

_____

_____

_____

_____

_____

_____

_____

Who or what do you most often blame for your past or current struggles? Even if external factors played a role, what can you take personal responsibility for? How did you contribute to the situation? And what can you do to make things better going forward?

_____

_____

_____

_____

_____

_____

_____

_____

_____

_____

_____

_____

I can create my own luck in life by . . .

_____

_____

_____

_____

_____

_____

_____

_____

_____

_____

_____

_____

Today, make note of any time you're tempted to blame someone or something else instead of doing something hard, such as blaming someone for "making" you feel uncomfortable instead of setting a boundary or blaming bad luck for a missed opportunity instead of acknowledging where you fell short. Then consciously choose to do the hard thing, or take a baby step in that direction, and write about your experience. Was this challenging? Empowering? Any aha moments?

_____

_____

_____

_____

_____

_____

_____

_____

_____

Write a poem titled "I'm Done Waiting" that explores why and how you'll be more proactive in an area of your life where you've been waiting for things to change. The poem doesn't have to be long. It doesn't have to rhyme. Just write from your heart and let your creative juices flow.

_____

_____

_____

_____

_____

_____

_____

_____

_____

_____

Draw yourself as a puppet and a large pair of scissors cutting the strings. Along each string, write one thing you will no longer allow to control you.

FOSTERING OPTIMISM

Optimist: Someone who figures
that taking a step backward
after taking a step forward
is not a disaster, it's a cha-cha.

—ROBERT BRAULT

Write any defeatist, negative thoughts you've been having about a challenge you're currently facing. Then reframe each thought to something more empowering and note how that changes your feelings about the situation, and consequently, how you might handle things going forward. For example, instead of telling yourself, "Things will never get better," you could think, "I'm learning and growing every day, and will see progress if I keep at it."

What fears do you currently hold about your future, and what would you need to trust or believe to view your future more optimistically?

_____

_____

_____

_____

_____

_____

_____

_____

_____

_____

_____

_____

I know I can make the best of anything that happens because . . .

_____

_____

_____

_____

_____

_____

_____

_____

_____

_____

_____

Every time you're tempted to complain today, identify one positive thing about the person or situation and either jot them down here as you go or come back to this page at the end of the day to reflect on your experience. Note how reframing your complaints affected your mood and your choices.

_____

_____

_____

_____

_____

_____

_____

_____

_____

_____

Do a word-association exercise starting with the word "optimism." Write the next word that comes to mind, then the next, then the next. Don't overthink it or censor yourself—just write and see where the exercise takes you. When your mind is clear, review the list and write down anything you learned about yourself, your past, your fears, or your beliefs through this experience.

_____

_____

_____

_____

_____

_____

_____

_____

_____

_____

Draw your brain when you're thinking optimistic thoughts, including images, words, or both.

FACING YOUR FEARS

F-E-A-R has two meanings:
"Forget Everything And Run"
or "Face Everything And Rise."
The choice is yours.

—ZIG ZIGLAR

Think about a time when you were afraid to do something that would have been life-enhancing for you but you pushed through fear and were ultimately glad you did. Note below what your fear was trying to protect you from and why you didn't actually need that protection.

How has fear held you back in life, and who might you become if you challenged yourself to take action, even if only through baby steps, in spite of your fears?

_____

_____

_____

_____

_____

_____

_____

_____

_____

_____

_____

_____

Sometimes, when the things we fear might happen actually happen, it's for the best because ...

_____

_____

_____

_____

_____

_____

_____

_____

_____

_____

_____

_____

_____

Do something small (or large!) to face one of your biggest fears today. Write about what this experience was like for you. What did you do? What happened as a result? Did you learn anything that can help you going forward?

Think about an encounter or conversation you fear having—a job interview, a heart-to-heart with a relative or your significant other—and imagine you are able to read the other person's mind. Now imagine that some of their thought processes are similar to your own, because they too are human and likely have many of the same fears. Write their inner dialogue, including their worries and concerns about this conversation with you, then note whether it eases your fears to consider that they too might feel scared.

Draw a bottle that contains the antidote to fear and list on the label all the active ingredients.

EMBRACING
VULNERABILITY

You don't need to pretend to be okay when you're not okay. Can we stop reserving the word "strong" for people who "power through" and "get on with it" when what they really need is support and compassion? It takes true strength to be vulnerable and honest about your emotions.

—MEGAN ROSE LANE

List any fears that prevent you from being vulnerable with other people and sharing your feelings and struggles. For each, give one reason to push through your fear, and one thing you can do or tell yourself if this is hard for you.

_____

_____

_____

_____

_____

_____

_____

_____

_____

_____

_____

_____

Think about a time when you opened up to someone about something painful or challenging and then felt glad you did. What did you share? How did they respond? How did this help, encourage, or empower you? And did you learn anything that might help you continually embrace vulnerability in the future?

_____

_____

_____

_____

_____

_____

_____

_____

_____

_____

_____

_____

Growing up in my family, I learned that vulnerability . . .

_____

_____

As a result of what I learned growing up, I now . . .

_____

_____

_____

If I want to be more vulnerable now, I know I need to . . .

_____

_____

_____

I can work on this by . . .

_____

_____

_____

Tell someone you feel safe around something you're tempted to keep inside today—share a thought, opinion, feeling, or memory you might otherwise hide in shame or fear. Write about what this was like for you. How did you feel before? And after? How did the person respond? Did it enable you to connect on a deeper level?

_____

_____

_____

_____

_____

_____

_____

_____

_____

_____

_____

Imagine you could go back in time and write a graduation speech for your own graduating class that starts with this Brené Brown quote from her bestselling book *Rising Strong:* "People who wade into discomfort and vulnerability and tell the truth about their stories are the real badasses." Explain why vulnerability is a sign of strength, and focus on all the things younger you and your peers will gain if you find the courage to be vulnerable.

_____

_____

_____

_____

_____

_____

_____

_____

_____

_____

Draw the cover of the book containing your life story, told with rawness and authenticity.

ACCEPTING EMOTIONAL DISCOMFORT

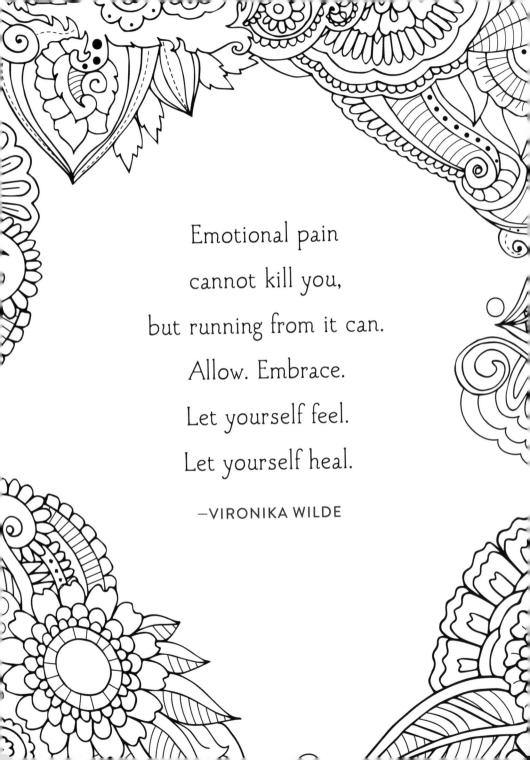

Emotional pain
cannot kill you,
but running from it can.
Allow. Embrace.
Let yourself feel.
Let yourself heal.

—VIRONIKA WILDE

Write about a time when you did something you later regretted so you could avoid sitting with an uncomfortable feeling. Empathize with yourself instead of judging yourself, and list anything you learned from the experience.

_____

_____

_____

_____

_____

_____

_____

_____

_____

_____

_____

What emotion do you find most uncomfortable and often resist? Why does this emotion make you uncomfortable? How has your resistance impacted you and your life? And what might change if you allowed yourself to embrace this emotion instead?

It's safe to allow myself to feel emotional pain because . . .

_____

_____

_____

_____

_____

_____

_____

_____

_____

_____

_____

_____

_____

Today, whenever you feel a strong emotion, take a five-minute (or longer) pause before taking any action. Simply sit with the feeling, noting any physical sensations in your body and fear-based thoughts running through your mind. Return to this page at the end of the day to explore what this experience was like for you and what, if anything, you learned.

Write a dating profile for an emotion you often resist, focusing on why this emotion needs and deserves love, empathy, and attention.

Draw a "license to feel," similar to a driver's license, and include all emotions you're allowed to simply feel without having to fight them, numb them, or act on them.

Building Inner Strength Physically

When we think of inner strength, we often think of it as an inside job, entirely dependent on our thoughts, feelings, and perceptions, but our physical choices play a huge role as well. If we squeeze fast-food meals into a crammed schedule, spend all our time with people who drain and discourage us, and surround ourselves with chaos and clutter, we'll always feel depleted and overwhelmed. And if we refuse to create space in our packed planner for self-care and enjoyment—zoning out with booze and other bad habits in our limited free time to avoid facing ourselves—we're even more likely to feel sapped and stressed. Our relationships, our environment, the things we consume—they all impact how we feel and how well we're able to handle our daily stressors. That's what this section is all about.

The following pages cover seven different types of physical habits and choices that help us feel our strongest:

- **Taking care of yourself,** so you can honor your physical needs, adopt a healthy diet and exercise routine, and get enough sleep to function at your best.
- **Constructing your ideal environment,** so your home feels peaceful, joyful, and energizing.
- **Creating a circle of allies,** so you surround yourself with people who uplift, support, and encourage you.

- **Changing your relationship to technology,** so you don't feel drained by your tech use or discouraged by social media.
- **Becoming conscious of what you consume,** so you're not negatively affected by the media and ads you consume daily.
- **Preparing for busy times,** so you have a plan to deal with them and even thrive, instead of feeling stressed, overwhelmed, and overloaded when your responsibilities pile up.
- **Making time for passions,** so you make time for the things that make you feel fulfilled and alive, which lowers your stress and boosts your happiness.

This section is all about consciously choosing who you allow around you and what you let get inside you. It's about doing the things that build you up, knowing what sustains you, and avoiding what drains you. It's also protecting your energy and attention—two of your most valuable commodities—especially when life feels so fast and fierce that it's hard to slow down and check in with yourself. You have the power to fuel and fulfill yourself by developing good physical habits—you just need to take a step back and recognize what brings out the best in you and what makes you feel your worst. So take a deep breath, grab your pen, and get ready to connect the dots.

TAKING CARE OF YOURSELF

I have come to believe that caring
for myself is not self-indulgent.
Caring for myself is an act of survival.

—AUDRE LORDE

Describe your current diet/exercise routine below. Note whether it nourishes or drains you and what you'd need to change to feel and be your physical best. Think in terms of small but manageable shifts—little things you can easily incorporate into your day without feeling overwhelmed.

_____

_____

_____

_____

_____

_____

_____

_____

_____

_____

_____

What helps you get a good night's sleep? If you don't currently sleep well, what could you do differently to ensure you get to bed at a decent hour, feeling relaxed, and sleep enough hours to function optimally the next day?

To make my physical self-care a top priority, I need to stop . . .

_____

_____

_____

I need to start . . .

_____

_____

_____

I need to believe . . .

_____

_____

_____

I need to set boundaries with/around . . .

_____

_____

_____

Once every hour today, check in with yourself to gauge your physical needs. If you've been sitting and feel sore, get up and walk for a few minutes. If your head hurts, drink a glass of water. If your hands feel tense from typing, give yourself a quick hand massage. Write about what you did to meet your needs throughout the day, anything you learned from this experience, and what your life might be like if you did this regularly going forward.

Think about the part of your body that feels the weakest or most pained, either from overuse or injury. Now imagine this body part brought you to a therapy session to tell you its deepest feelings and needs. What does it tell you? What does it want you to know? What does it wish you'd do or not do going forward?

_____

_____

_____

_____

_____

_____

_____

_____

_____

_____

Draw something related to your favorite physical self-care ritual.

CONSTRUCTING YOUR
IDEAL ENVIRONMENT

When a flower doesn't bloom,
you fix the environment in which
it grows, not the flower.

—ALEXANDER DEN HEIJER

Describe your ideal home environment, factoring in what helps you feel calm, balanced, and connected to yourself. Note anything you'd need to add, change, or remove from your current environment to get closer to this ideal.

_____

_____

_____

_____

_____

_____

_____

_____

_____

_____

_____

What are some physical things you've held on to—perhaps for nostalgia's sake or simply attachment—that don't fuel you in any way, and maybe even bring you down? What would you need to believe or stop believing to let these things go, and how might your life change if you did?

It drains me when I surround myself with . . .

_____

_____

_____

_____

_____

_____

I feel like my best self when I surround myself with . . .

_____

_____

_____

_____

_____

_____

Set an intention based on how you want to feel today—calm, confident, or motivated, for example. Add one thing to the space where you'll spend most of your time today that supports this intention. This might mean a candle with a soothing scent, a sticky note with a motivational quote, or even a new playlist that energizes you. Write about what this experience was like for you. How did it impact your mood? Your thoughts? Your feelings? Your actions? If it had no impact, why do you think that is?

_____

_____

_____

_____

_____

_____

_____

_____

Imagine you're about to spend a week in a minimalistic log cabin, with only the basic necessities and a beautiful natural environment outside your door. Write about what it's like to wake up, work, relax, and go to sleep within this sparse space, and how it affects your state of mind.

_____

_____

_____

_____

_____

_____

_____

_____

_____

_____

Channel your inner Marie Kondo (the bestselling author and organizing guru) and draw a physical possession that sparks joy.

CREATING YOUR
CIRCLE OF ALLIES

Little by little I will dig myself out,
but the task is so much easier
when people are offering me a hand
and cheering me on
as I climb back up to the light.

—SARAH WHITE

List all the qualities that you believe make someone a good friend. Then note who in your life (if anyone) has these qualities and how they help you be your best self. If you don't have anyone like this in your life—or not many people—write what you'd need to believe, do, or stop doing to change this.

_____

_____

_____

_____

_____

_____

_____

_____

_____

_____

_____

If author and motivational speaker Jim Rohn was right and you are the average of the five people you spend the most time with, what does this say about you? How do the five people you currently spend the most time with influence and impact you, for better or worse?

_____

_____

_____

_____

_____

_____

_____

_____

_____

To increase my time around people who uplift, encourage, and support me, I would need to . . .

_____

_____

_____

_____

_____

_____

_____

_____

_____

_____

_____

_____

Today, identify one way you can be the kind of friend you want to have, and one or more things you can do to show it in action—then do it. Write about what this was like for you. What did you choose? What did you do? How did this feel? How did people or the other person respond?

_____

_____

_____

_____

_____

_____

_____

_____

_____

_____

_____

Imagine you wake up with an inescapable compulsion to tell everyone the truth, and you then get stuck in an elevator with someone who put you down in the past, perhaps regularly. What you would say to them about how they impacted you, why they were wrong, and how you deserve to be treated?

_____

_____

_____

_____

_____

_____

_____

_____

_____

_____

Reflect on the idea of "holding space" for someone who's going through hard times, which essentially means being present and listening without judgment. Now draw the metaphorical "space" you'd want someone to hold for you, and if you feel so inclined, draw someone in your life who excels at providing this kind of support.

CHANGING YOUR RELATIONSHIP TO TECHNOLOGY

Almost everything will work again

if you unplug it for a few minutes,

including you.

—ANNE LAMOTT

Today, whenever you're about to pick up your phone without a clear motivation, record here what you're feeling—for example, lonely, bored, overwhelmed, or insecure. Then identify one thing you can do to address your emotions/what you need, instead of using technology as a crutch.

_____

_____

_____

_____

_____

_____

_____

_____

_____

_____

In what way does technology enrich you? In what way does it drain you? And what could you do to increase the former and decrease the latter?

_____

_____

_____

_____

_____

_____

_____

_____

_____

_____

If I didn't compare myself to people on social media, I would . . .

_____

_____

_____

_____

_____

_____

_____

_____

_____

_____

_____

_____

_____

Spend at least one hour tech-free today. Put your phone/tablet away, turn off the TV, and do something that energizes you instead. Write about what this was like for you. What did you feel? What did you think? What did you do? Was this hard for you? Or enjoyable?

_____

_____

_____

_____

_____

_____

_____

_____

_____

_____

_____

Imagine you're snowed in at your home with your closest loved ones for a full day (or longer!), without any access to technology. There's no electricity, no internet, all batteries have died. How would you connect with yourself and the people around you? How might this differ from the usual time you spend alone or with the people you love?

Draw a smartphone and include app icons for all the things that make you feel your strongest and best (for example: nature, yoga, or healthy food).

BECOMING CONSCIOUS OF WHAT YOU CONSUME

Your diet is not only what you eat. It's what you watch, what you listen to, what you read, the people you hang around . . . be mindful of the things you put into your body emotionally, spiritually, and physically.

—UNKNOWN

List the top media sources/content you consume on a regular basis, including TV shows, podcasts, email newsletters, blogs, YouTube videos, music, and social media platforms. For each, note your top motivation for consuming this content—what needs you're trying to meet, such as entertainment, distraction, or education—and whether it impacts you positively or negatively. Do these sources align with your values and goals? Do they make you feel better or worse about yourself? Do they enhance your life or deplete you?

How does advertising, on TV and online, impact your self-esteem and spending habits? Do you often buy things you don't need to feel better about yourself because of the ads you consume? How might it impact you for the better if you minimized your exposure to ads?

I know I've spent too much time online when ...

_____

_____

_____

_____

_____

_____

Instead of mindlessly consuming content on the web, I could enrich myself by ...

_____

_____

_____

_____

_____

_____

Today, during a time when you would usually consume some sort of media, binge-watch something in the natural world. For example, take a walk with the intention of noticing interesting trees, or spend a while staring at a lake or watching an animal play. Then return to this page to record what this was like for you. Was it hard? Was it a positive experience? Why or why not? How did it impact your state of mind?

_____

_____

_____

_____

_____

_____

_____

_____

_____

_____

Write a mass text you'd send to every contact in your phone if you decided to no longer respond to messages instantly or quickly going forward. Then write how it might it benefit you and improve your life if you stopped being instantly available.

_____

_____

_____

_____

_____

_____

_____

_____

_____

_____

_____

_____

Draw a morning or presleep activity that would be more nourishing than scrolling on your phone.

PREPARING FOR
BUSY TIMES

Busy people make
"to-do" lists when
what they need is to reflect
and create "stop-doing" lists.

—FRANCIS SHENSTONE

Write about a time when life got busy and you felt stressed and overwhelmed. What helped you during this time? What hurt you during this time? What, if anything, did you learn about yourself, your choices, and your needs?

_____

_____

_____

_____

_____

_____

_____

_____

_____

_____

_____

_____

What are some simple ways you can practice self-care when life gets busy so you can ensure you don't get depleted?

If you have an hour:

_____

_____

_____

_____

If you have a half hour:

_____

_____

_____

_____

If you only have five minutes:

_____

_____

_____

I feel my best when I make sure I am never too busy to . . .

_____

_____

_____

_____

_____

_____

_____

_____

_____

_____

_____

_____

Create a to-be list for your day, noting how you'd like to show up in the world. For example, you might want to be compassionate, present, and/or calm. Check in with yourself throughout your day, especially when you feel busy or overwhelmed, to see what you need to do or not do to honor your intentions. At the end of the day, write about what this experience was like for you and what, if anything, you learned.

_____

_____

_____

_____

_____

_____

_____

_____

_____

_____

Write yourself a permission slip for busy times, including what you have permission *to do* and *not to do*.

_____

_____

_____

_____

_____

_____

_____

_____

_____

_____

_____

_____

Draw a clock set to a time of day that you can devote to reconnecting with yourself, no matter how busy life gets. Around it, write—or draw images to represent—all the things you can do at this time.

MAKING TIME
FOR PASSIONS

You know how every once in a while you do something and the little voice inside says, "There. That's it. That's why you're here." . . . and you get a warm glow in your heart because you know it's true? Do more of that.

—JACOB NORDBY

Reflect on a hobby or activity that puts you in a good mood and enables you to be your best self. Why do you enjoy it? How does it enrich or fulfill you? Do you regularly prioritize this? Why or why not?

_____

_____

_____

_____

_____

_____

_____

_____

_____

_____

_____

_____

_____

What are some activities you enjoyed as a kid? Which of these things do you still do now, and which have you stopped doing that you might want to resume?

_____

_____

_____

_____

_____

_____

_____

_____

_____

_____

_____

I need and deserve to prioritize my passions because . . .

Make a list of activities you've never tried that excite you (the more, the better!). Pick one to try today and then write about your experience—what you did, with whom (if anyone), and how it impacted you physically, mentally, and emotionally.

_____

_____

_____

_____

_____

_____

_____

_____

_____

_____

_____

_____

Imagine you hired a private detective to follow you for the day and report back on any physical or mental habits that might be getting in the way of your ability to prioritize and enjoy the activities you love. Write their report, including recommendations for improvement.

Draw a tool kit for a hobby you're passionate about, including anything physical, mental, or emotional that you need to enjoy this activity and get into a state of flow.

Building Inner Strength Spiritually

Whether you identify as spiritual or religious—or perhaps neither—there are certain practices that fall under each umbrella that fuel us when all else fails. When your mind is too loud and your heart is too heavy and your body feels weak and drained, leaning on your spiritual practice can help you access a transcendent strength within that helps you rise above it all. You don't have to have faith in God or go to church or believe in a personified universe that has your back. (I don't do any of these things, but if you do, more power to you!) Anything that deepens your connection with your higher self and what you consider sacred can be a spiritual practice. The following pages focus on some of the most popular practices:

- **Practicing mindfulness,** so you can get out of your head and stay in the now instead of draining yourself with worries, regrets, and judgments.
- **Connecting to something greater than yourself,** so you can feel more supported through life's challenges, whether it's through a higher power, the universe, or spiritual/religious practices.
- **Finding meaning in adversity,** so you can better accept your struggles by finding a greater purpose behind every obstacle.
- **Learning to let go and trust,** so you can relax into the flow of life and accept each challenge as it comes instead of doubting yourself and trying to control everything.

- **Choosing forgiveness,** so you can heal yourself and your relationships and release the heavy burden of anger and resentment.
- **Getting outside yourself,** so you focus less on your own wants and problems, and help both yourself and others by giving back.
- **Communing with nature,** so you can find peace, calm, and healing in the natural world, away from the hectic pace of your daily life.

This section is all about enlightening and empowering yourself through both *less* and *more*—less distraction, less destruction, less self-obsession; more reflection, more connection, more decompression. It's about healing your spirit, hearing your inner wisdom, and creating your own blueprint for presence and peace—the good stuff you were born with before your pain convinced you to armor up and shut down. So take a deep breath, grab your pen, and get ready to chart your way home.

PRACTICING
MINDFULNESS

If you want to conquer the
anxiety of life, live in the moment,
live in the breath.

—AMIT RAY

Take a little time to check in with your senses to pull yourself out of your head and into your body. Then list:

Five things you see:

_____

_____

Four things you can touch:

_____

_____

Three things you can hear:

_____

_____

Two things you can smell:

_____

_____

One thing you can taste:

_____

What is the story you are telling yourself right in this moment about anything frustrating or stressful going on in your life? Become the observer of your thoughts and identify the narrative you're spinning, including any assumptions, judgments, and projections that might be clouding your vision and preventing you from responding to reality as it actually is.

_____

_____

_____

_____

_____

_____

_____

_____

_____

_____

_____

I feel most present in the moment when I . . .

_____

_____

_____

_____

_____

_____

I can integrate this into my daily life by . . .

_____

_____

_____

_____

_____

_____

Today, whenever you're talking to someone, focus solely on their words without reading into them or preparing your response in your head. Breathe through the instinct to interrupt or argue, and allow yourself to simply hear their words with an open, receptive mind. If intrusive thoughts pull you out of the moment, allow them to pass through without attaching to them and bring your focus back to your breath and the person in front of you. Write about what this was like for you. Did you find it challenging? Or rewarding? Did anything surprise you about this experience?

Make a list of things that you love and enjoy that are worth being fully present for.

_____

_____

_____

_____

_____

_____

_____

_____

_____

_____

_____

_____

Draw shapes, lines, and patterns using your nondominant hand. Focus on the feeling of your fingers on your writing utensil, the sound of it moving along the page, and the sensation of movement in your wrist. Practice non-judgment as you go. There are no mistakes, just opportunities for a more surprising, interesting drawing.

CONNECTING TO SOMETHING GREATER THAN YOURSELF

Some people "trust the universe,"
some "let go and let God," some find
strength in nature. It doesn't matter
what you believe, so long as your beliefs
harm none and help you find
the will to go on.

—ELLI LOVE

Write about your religious or spiritual beliefs/practice. Which rituals support your practice? How do they help, nourish, or strengthen you? Do you regularly prioritize them? Why or why not?

_____

_____

_____

_____

_____

_____

_____

_____

_____

_____

_____

What does spiritual growth mean to you, and what do you do (or could you do) to support your own spiritual growth?

_____

_____

_____

_____

_____

_____

_____

_____

_____

_____

_____

My higher self (or soul or Buddha nature) wants me to know . . .

_____

_____

_____

_____

_____

_____

_____

_____

_____

_____

_____

Think of someone who embodies all the qualities you aspire to possess. This could be a spiritual teacher, historical figure, or someone in your life, past or present. Whenever you're confronted with a difficult situation today, no matter how minor, ask yourself, "What would _____ do?" Write about what this was like for you. What challenges did you encounter? How did you respond? How did this differ from how you usually would?

Write a spiritual mission statement—a personal declaration of your values and your main purpose in life—to help guide you and support you through hard times.

_____

_____

_____

_____

_____

_____

_____

_____

_____

_____

_____

_____

Draw an animal that you consider a spiritual teacher, and if you feel so inclined, jot down on the page any lessons you've learned from this guide.

FINDING MEANING
IN ADVERSITY

Someday this pain
will be useful to you.

—PETER CAMERON

Write about the hardest time in your life and list everything you gained because of what you went through. Think of the qualities and/or skills you nurtured, lessons you learned, and unexpected blessings you received to find a deeper meaning in your experience.

_____

_____

_____

_____

_____

_____

_____

_____

_____

_____

_____

_____

_____

Would you be willing to make sacrifices in the short term for long-term gain for yourself or someone you love? Is it possible that something you're struggling with now might be such a sacrifice? If so, how? If not, have any past sacrifices benefited you or someone you love?

_____

_____

_____

_____

_____

_____

_____

_____

_____

_____

_____

If it weren't for the painful things in life, we might not appreciate . . .

Today, help someone with something you've struggled with so that you're recycling your pain into something useful. For instance, if drinking has been an issue for you, offer advice or support to someone in an online forum for alcoholism. Write about what you did, the impact you made, and how it felt to give your pain new meaning.

Write your eulogy from the perspective of someone who was inspired by your strength throughout your life and how far you came from where you started.

Draw something you have faith in or something that gives you hope.

LEARNING TO LET GO
AND TRUST

You're afraid of surrender because
you don't want to lose control.
But you never had control.
All you had was anxiety.

—ELIZABETH GILBERT

List any fears that prevent you from trusting in yourself and the future, and for each, one reason you can let that fear go.

_____

_____

_____

_____

_____

_____

_____

_____

_____

_____

_____

_____

In what area of your life are you currently trying to exert the most control? How is this draining you? And what would it look like to let go and let life happen?

_____

_____

_____

_____

_____

_____

_____

_____

_____

_____

_____

I trust that I can handle whatever comes at me, because I've survived a lot, including . . .

_____

_____

_____

_____

_____

_____

_____

_____

_____

_____

_____

_____

Identify one thing you would do or try if you trusted in yourself and the unknown, and take one small step toward that goal today. Write about what you did, how you feel, what excites you about this possibility, and how you can benefit from both the worst and best possible outcomes.

_____

_____

_____

_____

_____

_____

_____

_____

_____

_____

Your great-great-grandchild has just found a "letting go" time capsule you buried with physical items that represent things in your life that worry or drain you. Describe what's in the box, what it represents, and why you chose to let it go.

_____

_____

_____

_____

_____

_____

_____

_____

_____

_____

_____

Draw an extended hand letting go of control, either the word itself or something that visually represents it.

CHOOSING FORGIVENESS

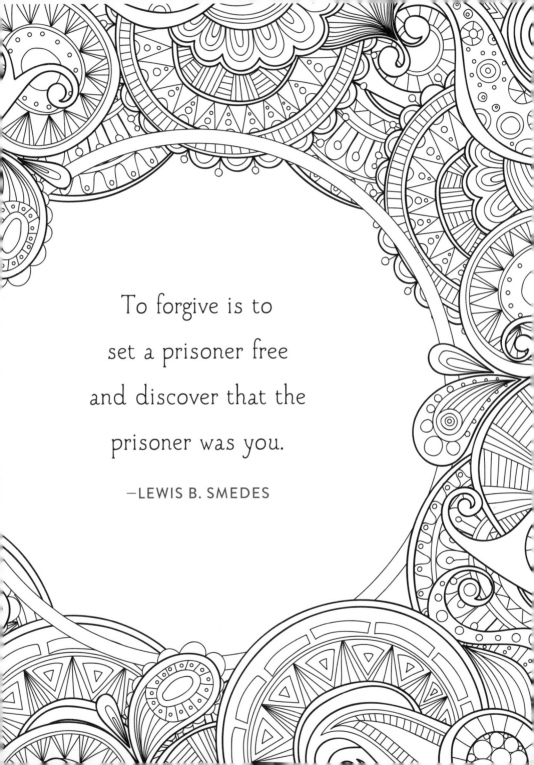

To forgive is to
set a prisoner free
and discover that the
prisoner was you.

—LEWIS B. SMEDES

Think of someone you've had a hard time forgiving and write about why this has been challenging for you. Then try to shift your perspective and explore why they might have done what they did, assuming that, at the time, they were doing their best based on their life experiences, perspective, challenges, and limitations. If it's too difficult to imagine they did their best, assume that "hurt people hurt people" and write about what pain may have compelled them to do what they did. Then list at least one positive thing you gained because of what you endured.

_____

_____

_____

_____

_____

_____

_____

_____

Do you think you're more forgiving toward yourself or others, and why? What would you need to believe to offer yourself and others the same level of forgiveness? How might it affect you and your life for the better if you did?

_____

_____

_____

_____

_____

_____

_____

_____

_____

_____

_____

When it feels hard to forgive, I need to remember . . .

Make "just like me" your mantra today and repeat this to yourself whenever someone upsets or annoys you. Driver cuts you off? "You get anxious and impatient, just like me." Coworker dominates a meeting? "You get insecure and feel a need to prove yourself, just like me." Instead of assuming the worst of the other person, try to recognize a potential shared struggle behind their actions to help soften your anger and forgive. Write about what this was like for you. Did you feel and respond differently than usual? Did this positively impact you or your day in other ways?

_____

_____

_____

_____

_____

_____

_____

_____

_____

Write a confession for something you've done that hurt someone else, apologizing without making excuses, to release the weight of guilt, shame, and/or regret.

Draw your inner child—in need of love, understanding, empathy, and support—and refer to this image often as a reminder to be gentle with yourself.

GETTING OUTSIDE YOURSELF AND HELPING OTHERS

The best way to forget about
your own problems is to help
someone else solve theirs.

—NORMAN VINCENT PEALE

Think about a time when you helped someone else or devoted yourself to a cause larger than yourself. How did you feel during and after? Did this help you as well as the person or people you helped? If so, what did you gain from the experience?

What do you believe is the greatest nonphysical gift you can give another person? When was the last time you gave this gift, and how could you do this more often going forward?

_____

_____

_____

_____

_____

_____

_____

_____

_____

_____

_____

_____

If I could do one only thing to help make the world a better place, I would focus my energy on . . .

Create a list of little things you could do to make a positive difference within your sphere of influence—activities that don't require much time or any special resources but could have a huge impact, nonetheless. Pick one thing to do today, then write about your experience and anything you gained, learned, enjoyed, or appreciated.

Pick one item that you don't need or rarely use that you could donate to charity and write the story of where it ends up. Who receives it? Why did they need it? How does it help them and/or change their life?

_____

_____

_____

_____

_____

_____

_____

_____

_____

_____

_____

_____

Draw a map from Separateness to Love, with kindness "landmarks" (e.g.: listening, giving) along the way.

COMMUNING
WITH NATURE

And into the forest I go,

to lose my mind and find my soul.

—JOHN MUIR

Write about a time when nature helped calm your mind and/or heal your heart. Where were you? What did you do? What did you most enjoy? How did getting outside help you find clarity, peace, presence, or perspective?

_____

_____

_____

_____

_____

_____

_____

_____

_____

_____

_____

How much time do you currently spend in nature? If not as much as you'd like, how could you increase the time you spend connecting to the natural world, and how could you bring more of the natural world in your home and work environment?

_____

_____

_____

_____

_____

_____

_____

_____

_____

_____

_____

When I'm sitting in silence in nature, I remember that . . .

_____

_____

_____

_____

_____

_____

_____

_____

_____

_____

_____

_____

Make a list of natural items for a short scavenger hunt—a particular bird, a purple flower, or a heart-shaped rock, for example. Then take ten to twenty minutes to walk outside today, focusing your attention on your surroundings and seeing how many items you can find. Write about how it impacted your state of mind to take this mindful nature walk and list anything you gained or appreciated about this experience.

_____

_____

_____

_____

_____

_____

_____

_____

_____

_____

Imagine you're a bird flying high above the town where you live and you're only able to see beauty in the world below you. Your mind is free of all fears and worries; you're simply present to your surroundings. Describe what you feel, soaring among the clouds, and what you see with this unique power, far removed from everything that weighs you down.

_____

_____

_____

_____

_____

_____

_____

_____

_____

_____

_____

_____

_____

Draw your nature happy place—somewhere you go or can go to clear your mind and find peace whenever you're feeling stressed or overwhelmed by life.

Lori Deschene is the founder of Tiny Buddha, a self-help site that draws inspiration from thousands of contributors who share their stories and life lessons on the blog. She's the author of *Tiny Buddha's Gratitude Journal, Tiny Buddha's Worry Journal,* and more. Lori identifies as many things—an introvert, a highly sensitive person, a dreamer, and a work-in-progress, to name a few. She loves traveling with her boyfriend, reading true crime books in the tub, playing with her sons, and planning all the adventures she dreams of sharing with her family.